MW01602005

# Goodnight, Grown-up

Copyright © 2024 by Betsy Soloway-Aizley

First hardcover edition October 2024

Cover design by Simone Bordage
Author headshot by Coco Leialoha

ISBN/SKU: 979-8-218-45964-2 (hardcover)

Published by Betsy Soloway-Aizley

Just Because You're Old Does Not Mean Falling Asleep Has To Be Boring

*To my own anxious mind -
the mind too anxious to sleep, and just anxious
enough to write this book.*

*And Tina, for listening to these stories during
our therapy sessions.*

# Table Of Contents

# 'Caution! Contents May Be Hot.' - Beverage Warnings and How to Approach Them

Farmers, baristas, and babies are all part of the same subcategory of homosapien: the people whose opinions on milk really matter. My uncle, Charles, was both a farmer and a baby, not at the same time. The 'squares and rectangles' analogy applies to this kind of human, since every barista and farmer was once a baby, but not every baby is a barista or a farmer. There are ways in which being a baby and being a barista or a farmer are similar, though. Charles said time and time again that the reason he became a farmer was because of how much he enjoyed infancy.

My father, Raynold, was a triplet. Charles, Lewis, and he were born in a beautiful, sprawling city. It was one of those magnetic sort of cities, bright lights and idyllic streets making it impossible to leave. Our whole family has always loved Hartford Connecticut. When

Charles announced that he was buying a farm in the midwest, Raynold and Lewis supported his brother; they were triplets, afterall. Having shared the joys of infancy, the triplets all understood Charles's need to become a farmer. If it wasn't for the cafe that Raynold and Lewis opened in the heart of Hartford a year prior, in order to fulfill their own longing to be babies, the brothers would have joined Charles.

Their cafe was called *Coughee*, after their mother - my grandmother - named Riananca, who suffered from severe asthma. Lewis still manages *Coughee*, but my father ended up moving to Charles's midwest farm when my mother, Kitty, was pregnant with me. Because of this, my father, Raynold, has now identified with all three of the kinds of people within the 'Milk Matters' subcategory of homosapien: a baby, a barista, and a farmer. Charles and Lewis admire my father and his milky achievements, and turn to him for advice on how to approach milky matters.

Just days after Raynold's move to the midwest, Lewis had a customer at *Coughee* request for their latte to be extra hot. Lewis tried to advise them against it, explaining that overheating the milk may result in both burned hands and a foul taste, but the customer was steadfast in their decision. Lewis called my father, but Raynold was busy tending to a sore teat on our goat Cathy, so Lewis dealt with the customer on his own.

In hopes to be more environmentally friendly, *Coughee* switched the lids on their hot beverage cups from plastic to 100% recycled plastic. The downside to the new lids was that there was no temperature warning written on the top. When serving the customer their extra hot latte, Lewis decided to go into the back closet to find one of the last remaining old lids, one with a temperature warning. The customer said they were fine to wait a moment longer if it was for safety purposes.

Raynold called Lewis back after finishing with Cathy's teat, and was pleased with his brother's decision to use one of the older lids. Charles overheard his brothers' conversation and was overcome by a wave of pride. The triplets had so greatly enjoyed their time during infancy, and look at them now! Charles and Raynold were gathering milk, Lewis was serving milk, and all three of them had a true appreciation for what milk had to offer.

Riananca was never able to breastfeed, so the triplets relied solely on formula. Riananca made the experience the best it could have been for the boys, using only their favorite bottles and cycling through dozens of formula brands until she found one that all three infants enjoyed. She would be proud, oh so proud. She would also be rolling her eyes at a customer who thought they knew better than babies, farmers, and baristas.

# Bedskirt

I have finally chosen a bedskirt, after a month-long process. There are many variables to consider when finding the perfect bedskirt, such as spacing of the pleats and whether I want to still be able to see under my bed, having it fall just in line with the slats and sideboards, or touch the floor. Since my bedframe is a dark walnut, I also had to consider the level of contrast I wanted between the wood and the bedskirt. There are two sets of sheets that I alternate between, one beige and one cream. I knew I wanted a bedskirt that was somewhere in the middle of the two colors, so I wouldn't start to favor one set over the other. That's where the walnut came in, since it is much darker than my sheets. Luckily, both the beige and cream sheet sets have warm undertones, so I never had to consider a cool-toned bedskirt.

Home Depot's paint swatches came in handy throughout this process. I brought home squares of seventeen different options, ranging from beige to cream. After holding each one up to my dark walnut bed frame, I settled on one called Pale Dickcissel, but the decision was difficult. The swatches of Milk Dust and White Sands were close contenders.

I took my square swatch of Pale Dickcissel to T.J. Maxx to hold the color up to the various bedskirts. I knew I wanted to buy one in person, because of the color match, but mostly because of the pleat spacing. Hidden behind packages of duvet covers and throw blankets was my near-perfect match. On my way to the register, I realized I had forgotten to measure the distance between my bed's sideboards and the floor. I remembered the product identification number from my bedframe and searched online for the dimensions.

After comparing the measurements, I found that the bedskirt I chose would just graze the floor, if attached properly. The color was so perfect, identical to Pale Dickcissel, that the choice was made for me. In the end, it was clear that the bedskirt that is meant to be will be, and those decisions that had kept me up at night for the past four weeks were not in my control.

I immediately put my new bedskirt into the wash

when I got home, then hung it to dry so as to not shrink it at all. When it was time to dress my bed, I knelt beside my mattress, pressing my elbows into the dark walnut sideboards. That was the first time I ever prayed.

# Logging Out: How I Do It

In the top right corner of my screen, there is a little blue button. When I click on it, a drop-down menu appears, which leads to my account settings, payment details, FAQs, and 'log out.' Account settings is where I go when I want to reset my password or change the emoticon that appears next to my username. There is a limit on the amount of username resets - twice for free, but it gives the option to change it up to six times for a flat rate of $19.99. I created my account a few years ago, and luckily paid my dues back then, when the flat rate was only $17.99. I have changed my username five times since, and though it may seem like a waste of $17.99, I am not planning to utilize my final name change. I am satisfied with the username I landed on: RoxanneL.

The 'payment details' option in the little blue

button's drop-down menu shows the credit or debit card the website has on file, but displays only the last four digits. The other twelve digits are displayed using 'X.' Back when the flat rate for extensive username changes was $17.99 instead of $19.99, there was less attention to privacy, and the full card number was shown when 'payment details' was clicked. With the price change came the twelve Xs, though everybody's account updated this privacy setting regardless of whether or not they paid the flat rate. It is helpful that the last four digits are still shown, preventing any confusion over what card is on file. I updated my billing address through the payment details page a few months ago, when I moved from a two bedroom condo on Main Street to a three bedroom townhouse on Maine Street.

The Frequently Asked Questions page does not change much, proof of it being infrequently visited. If more people explored the FAQs tab, those questions would not be asked so frequently. There would even be space for new questions to be added, perhaps about the increased flat rate allowing six username changes, or the twelve Xs per card on file.

'Log Out' is listed at the bottom of the little blue button's drop-down menu, the last option of these four. I like to click on each before choosing to log out, making sure my emoticon feels accurate, and that my updated billing address is entered correctly. I check on the FAQs list to see if it has changed at all, so I can learn something new. Finally, I hover my mouse over the 'Log Out' button and click.

After logging out, it takes a second or two for the site to reload, which is just enough time for me to push my chair away from my desk. I am then brought back to the website's sign in page, where I type in my username and password, and start it all again.

# Sand In My Socks

I went to the beach last week to pick up my eldest son, Joshua. He had stayed at his friend's vacation home for the weekend, and packed one towel more than the number of days he was visiting. When I arrived at the beach, he had only used one of the towels he brought, the other two were still folded and dry. The towel he chose to use used to belong to his brother, but they traded towels a few summers ago, when they both started to like the other's towel better than their own.

The four of us - my husband, Alan, and our boys, Joshua and Nate - were going to the beach, a different beach than this one. Alan and I had to lay one of the back seats down in our Honda CR-V Hybrid, in order to fit our umbrella in the trunk. Joshua and Nate had to sit with their elbows touching, on the other side of the backseat, that we kept upright. The boys were fine with this; it made it easier for them to play on the iPad together. There was a lull in their gaming, and Alan was chewing a bagel.

As we finished pushing our umbrella into the sand, Alan asked me to rub sunscreen on his back. I said I would, since I had already finished applying sunscreen onto Joshua and Nate. The boys dug through my beach bag to grab their towels, and as they each unfolded theirs, Nate said that he liked how Joshua's towel looked, and Joshua said that Nate's towel looked nice too. Then Alan laughed, making the sunscreen smear a bit below his shoulder, since I was still rubbing it in. Joshua asked his dad what he was laughing about, and Alan told him that he and his brother should switch towels, and that the idea of them trading their towels was what made him laugh. Nate overheard this, and said that he would like to trade his towel with Joshua, and Joshua said he would too.

They both became attached to their newly traded towels, sleeping with them like blankets and using them after showers, so I was not surprised when that towel was the one Joshua used for his whole visit at his friend's vacation home. What was surprising, though, was how much sand was stuck on the wet towel when we put it in my car.

I brought a pair of sandals with me, in case I wanted to walk on the sand, as well as an extra pair of socks. My grandmother always told me to carry an extra pair of socks with me at all times; she said that they could be utilized in a multitude of ways. I was closer with my grandmother than anyone in the world, so I never questioned her.

Joshua's wet towel landed right on my extra pair of socks, but I did not think anything of it. Just this morning, I found myself needing new socks while at the grocery store, and felt grateful for my grandmother's fantastic idea. I grabbed my balled up socks from the back seat, which happened to be inside-out. Alan always stores socks inside-out, mine included. When I slipped them on, my feet felt sand on the inside, since that was where Joshua's towel landed a week prior. It made me think of the beach, and my boys, and Alan's laundry techniques. I rubbed my toes together and scrunched the sand in between.

# Bob's Shed

The five-by-four steel box belonged to the previous owners of Bob's house on Faded Valley Road. Susan and Janice, happily married mothers of two over 22, offered to dispose of the shed to make the move easier for Bob and his wife Martha. Martha told Susan and Janice they could leave the shed, since it seemed like the perfect storage for Bob's growing collection of shovels and hoes.

Martha never informed Bob of this conversation. She knew how much her husband loved surprises, and rolled all of Bob's shovels and hoes across the lawn, into the shed, in a rusty red wheelbarrow Susan and Janice also left for them. There were cobwebs in each corner of the shed, but it was otherwise completely empty. Martha did not have any paper towels or gloves with her, so she arranged Bob's shovels and hoes without removing the cobwebs first - she knew her husband would not mind.

On moving day, Bob and Martha drove their 2007 Buick Lucerne over to the new house before the movers arrived. They wanted to put milk and eggs in the fridge without any distractions. There is a perfect view of the shed when standing at the kitchen sink, so Martha suggested that Bob bring a few dirty plates over with them to wash. Bob thought that was a great idea, a perfect opportunity to get a sense of the water pressure they would soon be living with.

Susan and Janice left a bottle of dish soap behind the kitchen sink, so Bob and Martha wouldn't find themselves stranded with dirty dishes. Bob used this soap to wash the dirty plates, and once they were sufficiently clean, he looked out the window and saw the shed. "Darling, that shed is perfect for my shovels and hoes," he told Martha.

"I know, dear. Let's go check it out."

Bob and Martha left the plates to dry and headed out to the shed. When Bob opened the door to the steel box, he gasped. "Oh goodness, Martha. You arranged this, didn't you. What a fantastic surprise."

"I am glad you like it," Martha said. "Susan and Janice agreed to leave it for you. I told them that it would be the perfect place for you to store your shovels and hoes."

Bob kissed his wife on the cheek. He pulled her in for a hug.

The sun is blocked behind the clouds today, the sky a solid gray. Martha loved stormy weather - Bob remembers that from when they were teenagers. He makes sure to keep the door to his shed shut completely, not wanting his shovels and hoes to rust any further. Bob leans into his cane, bending to pick a handful of dandelions. He feels raindrops on his neck as he lays the flowers against the steel.

# Perforated Paper

My colleague wants to cut paper easily, whether or not she has scissors handy. We used to have a box of perforated paper at the office, behind the excess printer paper in the smallest storage closet in the East Wing. I took the last of the box home with me for crafting; I wanted to document my recipes. Due to their varying lengths and difficulties, note cards were sometimes too small, though I did not want to put the shorter recipes that *would* fit a note card onto paper that was so much larger than necessary.

Everytime I went into the smallest storage closet in the East Wing at work, I checked for the box of perforated paper, and counted how many sheets were left. The box held 200 sheets of perforated paper to start, then slowly crept down to 148 over the span of six months. I waited until it had been an additional three months without any decrease before taking the 148 sheets of perforated paper home with me.

It was a Thursday, the day that I took the 148 sheets of perforated paper home with me - I have always loved Thursdays. The funny thing about a sheet of perforated paper, more specifically, the perforated paper in this box, is that the perforation allows the number of pieces to change. The person who is counting the sheets of perforated paper may be counting each sheet as a whole, or each part sectioned off by perforation as its own sheet. When I began keeping a tally of the number of sheets, I promised myself to never change the way I count - it would be way too sneaky of me.

I won't say there was never any temptation, though. The day before the three month mark was hit, I started to get nervous. I had waited for what felt like forever, checking - sometimes multiple times a day - to make sure that there were no less than 148 sheets of perforated paper. When I was doing one final tally before heading home for the night, anticipating the Thursday ahead, two full sheets of perforated paper stuck together, bringing the total to 147. I was tempted, in that moment, to rip along one of the perforated lines on another sheet (each piece had perforation on two lines, dividing the full sheet into three even pieces), bringing the number back up to 148, if I used a different counting technique. After counting it all again, licking my fingers to assure no pieces were stuck together, I realized what had happened, and never had to change my technique for counting the perforated paper.

Ten years and 444 documented recipes later, I officially used up every piece of every perforated sheet of paper. It just so happened to be a Thursday when Annettonia asked if I knew if the office had any perforated paper. Just hearing the words come out of her mouth brought tears to my eyes. She asked what was wrong, if she said something that upset me. The tears dripped down my face, landing in a perfect line on the printer paper beneath us. The tear-moistened paper ripped right down the middle. Annettonia said that would work for today, and grabbed one of the pieces.

# Granola Bars In The Lobby

My tire pressure is low, despite there not being a hole. I know from prior experiences that very cold weather can cause significant drops in tires' PSI, and my mechanic confirmed that as the reasoning for my tire pressure light turning on. I have seen the same mechanic for years; we are quite fond of each other. The atmosphere in the auto repair shop is warm, much less sterile than the usual, and I truly feel comfortable leaving my car there for however long is needed. My neighbor, Ruth, recommended I bring my car to Wintergreen Radiator Grilles and Repairs when the passenger seat door got stuck.

From the moment I walked through the doors of WRG&R, I knew I had made the right choice, listening to Ruth. She is often difficult to listen to, given her soft, barely-audible voice. Some teenagers egged her house one time, and when she went to yell at them to get off of her property, what came out was only a whisper.

The lobby of Wintergreen Radiator Grilles and Repairs has a ripped, yet functional, dark green upholstered couch, a fake tree in a plastic pot, and a vintage-looking coffee table with rubber coasters. The table beside one arm of the couch is also vintage-inspired, and is topped with an acrylic container, always fully stocked with granola bars and Gatorade. Even though I am comfortable leaving my car at WRG&R for however long is needed, I always want to stay there for the duration.

The dark green upholstered couch has one section in the middle free from any rips, probably because sitting directly on the crack between cushions is undesirable to most, but not to me. The first time I experienced the lobby of Wintergreen Radiator Grilles and Repairs, I sat down on the crack between the cushions on the dark green upholstered couch, and sipped on a bottle of orange Gatorade. The memory remains so fondly in my mind, I cannot imagine visiting WRG&R and sitting anywhere but on that unsullied crack. This was the moment I first met my mechanic. This was the moment I first met Minty.

A calloused, greased with biofluids and car parts, welcoming hand reaches out to me. "Hi doll, I'm Minty. You must be the owner of that beauty over there."

"Yep, the Hyundai Elantra."

"Why don't you drive her into the garage, and I can give her body a peek."

"Sounds good. Thank you, Minty. I really like your lobby, and I think that it is very generous of you to offer granola bars and Gatorade for patient clients."

"Fuel helps with patience."

"Wow, Minty. That-" I had to take a long pause. "That is one of the most profound things I have ever heard."

"It's true, doll. Why don't you grab a granola bar just in case she needs some work done today."

Minty ran the calluses through her pixie cut; even the streak of purple was peppered with some grays. She handed me a chocolate chip oat bar. A bit of car -grime rubbed off onto the package, but I was feeling patient from the Gatorade.

Sadly, this morning, during my visit to WRG&R, it only took Minty fifteen minutes to locate the issue. I still had a quarter of a bottle of Gatorade left, and a small corner of the granola bar which I was saving to share with her. Instead, I popped the whole square in my mouth and washed it down with the last orange swig. I stepped up to Minty and my Hyundai Elantra. Minty said that she would hardly call the puncture a 'hole.' In fact, it was barely a leak. The nail had so completely punctured the rubber, that the rubber itself formed around it. It was such a tight fit, there was no seepage. It was only when the weather got cold, and the rubber contracted, that air began to leak out. Minty said that it could have been like this for weeks.

# Cook or Toss: Radish Greens

The word 'greens' has become its own class of vegetables, often generalizing those of the leafy variety. Many leafy greens can be prepared similarly, and the differences in their flavors are often overlooked - when cooked, that is. Radish greens, for instance, can mimic arugula, with a slight bitterness and notes of pepper. Though they might seem intimidating at first - especially if you are used to buying already trimmed radishes - cooking with radish greens is simple.

If someone were to hand you an arugula salad, having used this logic, replacing the arugula with radish greens, though both result in a peppery experience, you might feel alarmed. The differences in leafy greens are exposed when raw. The concept is similar to that of people's emotions; being raw equates to being vulnerable, raw emotion referring to an unyielded expression of your feelings.

Comparing humans to vegetables is an accurate depiction of societally-deemed flaws. You may choose carrots depending on their stems, favoring the unwithered and smooth. People try to preserve vegetables like they try to prevent their own aging, as if wrinkles make them unworthy rather than showcase their endurance. At the end of the day, no amount of retinol is going to save you from a car crash, and leafy greens are going to decay in the bottom of your vegetable drawer whether you like it or not. Some of the best recipes are created when the goal is, even more so than tasting good, clearing out the fridge. After slicing your radishes, perhaps spreading a bit of butter on them with a sprinkle of sea salt, you could toss the radish greens. You could follow all of the latest trends to erase the smile lines in the corner of your eyes. Just know that someone else at that very moment chose to cook their radish greens. Maybe they also used up the last remaining chunks of onion, and laughed so hard their eyes closed and their cheeks dimpled somewhere new.

# Where I Sit

Benches are very convenient, and quite common in both suburban parks and inner city streets. There is a bus stop half a mile away from my house on Stelluptin Lane, which I take to work three days a week. The two days that I do not take the bus to work, it is because I work from home. I bought a desk with adjustable height settings, giving me the option to either sit or stand during meetings, or while answering emails. If I press and hold on the button on the left side of my desk, it will save the height it is currently at, so the next time I press that button, it will go right back to where I want it - if I have raised or lowered it since then.

If my legs feel tired after standing at my desk for an extended period of time, I will lower it, pull my chair back underneath, and sit. It always feels nice to relax my knees and calves. Same thing goes for when I am waiting at the bus stop, or arriving at the bus stop after a day at the office. There are two benches directly where the bus pulls up, but an additional five benches are at the park just steps away, along with two year-round Adirondack chairs. I choose the Adirondack chairs when I want to sit down after arriving from a day at work, but I sit on the bench right by the bus if I am waiting for it to take me to work in the morning. The Adirondack chairs have a larger seat, so my toes don't touch the ground when I slide back as far as the seat allows. It feels like a breath of summertime and a mini vacation, no matter the season.

I actually use a folding chair instead of a wheelie chair at home, so I can more easily store it when I choose to stand. When I first bought my standing-desk, I still had a chair with wheels, but it was too bulky to move into the corner when the desk changed height, and the fabric on its seat was beginning to tear too. A hardware store downtown was having a semi-annual sale, so I took the bus there after checking on their website that they had folding chairs in stock. I made sure to get to the bus stop early, leaving time to sit on both an Adirondack chair in the park and a bench at the bus stop itself. It felt important to sit in two different areas, seated on varying materials, before choosing a folding chair at the hardware store. Especially since I never choose to sit on the bus.

# Caring For and Understanding Linen

When I asked the sales associate at Bloomingdales for confirmation that owning just one pair of 100% linen pants is allowed, she said that yes, of course it is. I have been hung up on that interaction ever since. She introduced herself as Zenovia Kuznetzov, making my response feel inferior. "My name is Sue."

"No last name," she demanded, rather than asking.

"I do have a last name."

Zenovia Kuznetzov motioned for the person waiting behind me to come to the register, handing me my receipt and my new pair of 100% linen pants. I thought of her during my whole bike ride back home, and everytime I have worn those linen pants over the past few months. The concept of 'pants' is one I get hung up on frequently, so my fixation on Zenovia Kuznetzov's comment on linen doesn't surprise me as much as it might surprise someone else.

There are always an even number of pants in my drawers, paying homage to their usual descriptor: pairs. I have two pairs of black leggings, two pairs of purple leggings, four pairs of light wash skinny jeans with rips on the right knee and left thigh, two pairs of medium wash, low-rise baggy jeans with slightly frayed edges and intentionally distressed back pockets, six pairs of gray sweatpants, and then my one, lone, linen pant.

Referring to my linen pant as a pair of linen pants implies that I have four pairs of black leggings, four pairs of purple leggings, four pairs of light wash skinny jeans with rips on the knee, four pairs of light wash skinny jeans with rips on the thigh, four pairs of medium wash, low-rise baggy jeans with slightly frayed edges and intentionally distressed back pockets, and twelve pairs of gray sweatpants, and that is just absurd.

Growing up, both of my parents worked full-time; my dad was a cardiologist, my mom a travel nurse. I was deemed 'independent' from a very young age - making myself dinner before I reached the double digits, brushing my teeth and washing my face and tucking myself into bed before my parents got home.

I managed the solitude by promising anything else in my possession that it would never have to be alone. When Zenovia Kuznetzov was ringing up my pants, she asked if I wanted a bag. I shook my head no, knowing that I would be too intimidated by the greatness of 'Kuznetzov' to ask her to print a second receipt, like I normally would. One receipt, one not-so pair of linen pants. *They will have each other.*

When the linen pants get dry-cleaned, I hold the receipt close, keeping my promise of company. I always put it right back into one of the front pockets when we pick the linen up and all go home together. The name tag hanging from the dry-cleaner plastic reads: *Sue Kuznetzov*, to make sure a piece of Zenovia walks home with us too.

# Waiting For The End

Beatrice-Marie got a call from her daughter last night, alerting her of Perry's baseball practice today at noon. "Surely Perry doesn't want his grandmother driving him to baseball practice," she told Dierdra.

"You are correct, though I have come down with a cough. When given the option, he said he would prefer to have his grandmother than his coughing mother."

"That makes sense, I suppose. You said practice starts at noon?"

"Yes."

"Is it still at SevenFly Park?"

"Yes. SevenFly is about fifteen minutes from our house, so maybe pick him up at 11:00?"

"Dierdra, then we would be arriving at baseball practice over half an hour early. How about I pick Perry up at 11:30?"

"No, Mom, the earlier the better. It is a fifteen minute drive when I am driving. With your age, it might be much longer."

"Ah, I see."

"No, I don't think you do see. Didn't you get new bifocal lenses in your glasses a few days ago? It takes a while to see properly with those."

"It definitely is a big adjustment."

Beatrice-Marie's optometrist told her for years that bifocal lenses would be the perfect investment, since she is constantly switching between her reading glasses and her distance glasses. She vocalized her fear of the adjustment period, the hindrance it would have on her life and daily whereabouts. Dr. Anchpulountski said that Beatrice-Marie's eyes adjusting to bifocal lenses are like buds in spring; the pollen count is a hindrance, but allows for months in bloom. She finally agreed.

"Perry," she heard Dierdra say, further from the phone. "Grandma is going to drive you to baseball practice tomorrow."

"Okay. But I can't be late." Perry's voice was muffled in the background.

"I told her to pick you up at 11:00 so you can get to SevenFly Park by noon."

"Okay," he said again.

Beatrice-Marie wakes up this morning three hours before her alarm clock. The moon is still up, so they look at each other for a while. She puts on her slippers and shuffles into the kitchen, not bothering to make her bed because she doesn't like to. Beatrice-Marie turns back to the moon while her coffee brews, and immediately looks away once realizing it had been staring at her this whole time. She tried to give the moon privacy, but that was not reciprocated. The clock on the stove reads 4:13. *I hope I have enough time to get ready before picking up Perry*, Beatrice-Marie thinks to herself.

Taking her coffee to the kitchen table, she runs through her list of morning tasks before leaving at 10:30 to get to Dierdra's house by 11:00. Luckily, she just lives around the block. Her tasks include finishing up her coffee, cleaning the mug, eating some yogurt, taking a shower, and getting dressed. It will be tight, so it is a good thing Beatrice-Marie woke up earlier than planned.

She walks out the door at 10:25, and pulls out of the driveway at 10:30. At 10:59, when she arrives at Dierdra's house around the block, she call her daughter through the dashboard, thankful once again

34

for her decision to try bifocal lenses, despite the still challenging adjustment period. Perry walks out of the front door before the phone rings twice, looking all grown up in his baseball uniform.

"How long does your practice go for?" Beatrice-Marie asks him as he buckles his seatbelt.

"Three hours."

"Oh, so it doesn't make sense for me to go all the way home."

They pull up to SevenFly Park at exactly noon. If Beatrice-Marie were to head home, she would just have to turn back around shortly after arriving. She did not bring a book, but does have her new bifocal glasses, meaning she can spend these three hours practicing seeing. With the upper half of her bifocal lenses, she can see Perry all the way in left field, his favorite position. She can also see the catcher, whose squat makes her knees hurt empathetically.

With the lower part of her bifocal lenses, Beatrice-Marie can read the numbers on my odometer, the 117,409 miles she has traveled. She can also see the little gas tank with an arrow that reminds the driver what side of the car needs to be pulled up to the pumps at gas stations. Thank goodness for that little arrow.

The lower part of her bifocal lenses also allows

for her to see the stitching in her steering wheel. It is gray, which Beatrice-Marie found quite enticing when choosing this specific Toyota Corolla. She still has an hour before Perry's baseball practice finishes, so she looks upwards through the top half of her bifocal lenses to see the playground behind the baseball diamond at SevenFly Park. There is a mother pushing her two children simultaneously on the swingset, one of them has a bandaid on his arm and the mother has bags under her eyes.

Beatrice-Marie checks her odometer once more, practicing the quick switch between near and far that bifocal lenses allow. Before she knows it, Perry is opening the door to her Corolla, sweaty and dusty.

"How was practice?"

"Long."

"Really? I felt like it flew by!"

"We ran overtime. It's 3:13."

"Well, let's get you home then."

They pull up to Dierdra's house at half past four. "Thanks for letting me drive you, Perry."

"You know, Grandma, I always get carsick. Except for when you drive me."

"Is that so?"

"Yeah. Coach told us today about a tournament

we have in Connecticut in a couple of months. He said they'll be a bus to take the whole team, but I was wondering if maybe you would drive me?"

"Of course I will drive you, Perry. I am just a little concerned about the short notice, if my tone seems unsure."

# Old Shampoo

Last night, I fell asleep at 10:45 post meridiem. I dreamt of mixed berry compote until waking at 2:03 ante meridiem to check the time. Something in my dreams always leads me to check the time, such as visiting a watch store or teaching toddlers how to read analog clocks. I usually fall asleep at 10:30, so it makes sense that those extra 15 minutes of being awake led me to oodles and oodles of mixed berry compote. Oodles and oodles. Oodles and oodles.

My wife, Marigold, and I share a conditioner, but we use different shampoos. Conditioner, due to its viscosity, always runs out before shampoo. With two people sharing the same conditioner in conjunction with the conditioner's viscosity, it sometimes feels like we go through a bottle every hour. We buy conditioner in a 40 ounce bottle, and then our individual shampoos are 20 ounces each. Marigold thought this was a brilliant mathematical plan, given that 20 is half of 40, and we each use half of the conditioner, so we will finish each bottle at the same time. That is when I explained the difference in viscosities to my wife, and she understood the flaws in her idea.

Before I met Marigold, back when I was still with my husband Donald, I went to sleep at 8:30 post meridiem. Donald was always in bed by seven, allowing him enough time for his breathing exercises before I arrived under the covers. Donald did not use conditioner - he rarely even used shampoo. He found an all-in-one dish soap/shampoo/conditioner/laundry detergent at our local natural foods store and that was it for him. Donald always smelled like onions.

The 40 ounce bottle of conditioner that Marigold and I share has a subtle oat scent. She uses a moisturizing olallieberry shampoo, but I prefer a strawberry shampoo made for children. Marigold opened her new olallieberry shampoo after using up the 20 ounce version of the shampoo version of our oat-scented conditioner. Marigold's new olallieberry shampoo is less clarifying than her previous oat shampoo, so last night she chose to shampoo twice, to be sure her scalp was sufficiently cleansed. I tried not to be impatient, but as usual, I kept checking the time. Even in my waking hours, I am constantly aware of what the clock says.

Not just clocks though - I am drawn to numbers like some people are drawn to diamonds. When Marigold proposed, I counted the seconds between her kissing me and slipping the watch onto my wrist. I never wanted an engagement ring.

# Post Office

The dark gray floor of our town's post office smells like paper. It is one of the few public spaces I have been to that is carpeted. The carpet is flattened from years of dropped envelopes and mailmen and local literary communicators, but personally, I would not even want a fluffy, shag carpet when sending off letters. The mayor is a frequent visitor of the post office; I often see him standing beside the self-service kiosk, with that muted, electoral half-smile that we all know and love.

Yesterday, the mayor started talking to me about my favorite stamps. I told him that if I am mailing a letter to a parent, grandparent, or cousin, I like to keep it simple and patriotic with an eagle with its wings spread wide. The mayor said that he understood. I then explained that if I am sending a letter to a sibling or a colleague or a friend - besides Sebastian or Distant Nelly - my choice of stamp has a nautical theme, be it a lighthouse or even a buoy. Again, the mayor said that he understood.

"What is your favorite type of stamp?" I asked the mayor.

"When I was a boy, my mother gifted me a set of Van Gogh stamps. I unfortunately lost them long ago, but they are still the best I have ever had. Those are my favorite for sure."

"But Mayor, you just told me your favorite set of stamps. What is your favorite stand-alone stamp?"

"One with an English Fir."

I nodded. "I really enjoy the dark gray carpet here. Do you?"

The mayor knelt to touch the floor, then gasped.

"What is it, Mayor, is everything okay down there?"

"I just was not expecting a texture such as this! Especially not at the local post office I am so well acquainted with."

I joined the mayor on the dark gray carpet, feeling the raised parts of the fabric, the little divots with paper dust embedded deep inside. A white piece of paper stuck out from the texture, just a corner, no more than a few millimeters. I tugged on it and wiggled out a whole sheet of stamps that had been worn so deeply into the crevice, like a fossil stuck in an iceberg. "Look what I found, Mayor!"

His electoral smile shifted to the joy of a little boy as he held the stamps. Almond Blossoms and a Café Terrace At Night and The Starry Night rested in his palm.

# Virginia Left Cheese Puffs In The Fridge

There are many kinds of cheesy snacks, but my household only buys shaved parmesan. My parents say that it is the most cost effective and versatile form of cheese, and I agree. Shaved parmesan can be used on pasta and any dish requiring a shakable parmesan, but it can also be consumed like chips. Shaved parmesan is already prepared, no knives required, meaning we save water too, not having to wash dishes whenever we want a cheesy delight.

Almost a decade ago, my two eldest siblings - the twins, Alaska and Dakota - came home from their first day of middle school looking flustered. "What's wrong, Twins?" I asked them.

"Some kids at school brought cloudy cheese to school," Alaska said.

"Cloudy cheese?"

"Cloudy, like, puffy and airy clouds," Dakota said.

"Ah, I see. That's interesting. Did you try the cloudy cheese?"

"Yes, we tried the cloudy cheese," the twins said in unison.

That was the last time we ever spoke of cheese other than shaved parmesan. Before I got the chance to ask them what the cloudy cheese tasted like, our parents walked into the kitchen to eat a few pieces of shaved parmesan.

When I started middle school two years later, I anticipated a cafeteria filled with cloudy cheese for weeks prior, eager to try some, but there was none to be found. Not on my first day, second day, or any day in the three years to follow, was there any sign of cloudy cheese in my middle school cafeteria.

The youngest of us four, Virginia, is my least favorite sibling. She was a mistake, born when Alaska and Dakota were in college, and I was studying for my SATs. She came out of the womb a nuisance, and has stayed that way ever since. The main problem I have with Virginia is that she does not eat cheese. She never grabs a piece of shaved parmesan to snack on, let alone top her spaghetti with it. I have sworn at her about it, said things like, "Fuck you, cheese-free

Virginia."

Tonight we are celebrating her 3rd birthday, and I am considering not eating dinner with my family. When I asked my parents to top her birthday cake with shaved parmesan, they told me that was spiteful and rude, so I have decided to take matters into my own hands.

"Excuse me, Alabama," Virginia says to me as I open the refrigerator.

"Pardon me, Virginia. Happy birthday to you."

"Thank you. I have been waiting for you to say that all day."

My hand freezes, hovering above the shaved parmesan. Suddenly, rather than focusing on ways that I can sabotage my three year old sister on her birthday, my mind shifts to a self-reflective state. *Why do I feel so much hate towards Virginia?* It cannot solely be because she does not like shaved parmesan like the rest of us. I ponder this all afternoon, all through the dinner that I wind up attending in our dining room.

After Virginia blows out the three candles on her cheese-less birthday cake, the twins stand to get themselves some shaved parmesan to put on their slices. I hear Alaska gasp, then Dakota. "What is it, Twins?" Dad asks them.

"There are Cheese Puffs in the fridge."

It has been years since I have thought about cheese other than shaved parmesan, and it has been a decade since Alaska and Dakota first taught me about cloudy cheese, which I can only assume is a similar concept to 'Cheese Puffs.'

"Alabama," Virginia turns to me, having completed her wish. "Those are my Cheese Puffs. I left Cheese Puffs in the fridge. I tried to put them in the pantry, but could not reach the shelves."

"Why are you telling me this, Virginia?"

"Because I don't want you to hate me anymore."

# The Joys of Counting

Counting is a great way to keep track of numbers. Even numbers, when added together, always result in an even sum. The sum of two or more odd numbers is not always odd, though. An even number plus an odd number always equals an odd number.

Anything can be counted. The number of cubicles in an office can be counted, and the number of pens in each cubicle can be counted. Pens and pencils can be counted to find the total number of physical writing instruments in the office, grouped as total pens plus total pencils, or total blue pens plus total black pens plus total mechanical pencils plus total No. 2 pencils.

Children can be counted; all humans can be counted. Age is a way of counting humans. Counting is a way to group people and things together.

Counting is a necessary part of music - the number

of beats per measure, or simply counting the musicians in so they know when to begin. Metronomes count the beats per second.

People plan their lives by counting. They will plan certain life milestones by the age they wish to be to have children or get married or graduate college. People also plan their careers by counting. The years of schooling certain careers require are counted, as well as the tuition per year. The total tuition for the total number of years in school is then compared to the projected salary of this career that said degree will potentially secure. People count the positive benefits and the negative consequences.

Counting does not guarantee a certain outcome when applied to life and unpredictable scenarios. The one thing counting can guarantee is itself - it will always be there, whether someone is counting pens in a cubicle, points on a graph, or the years until their child is off to college.

# The Treadmill On My Lawn

Connor is wearing flip-flops today. They are blue, with the Superman logo under his heels, perfectly matching his backpack. I asked him if he would rather wear a shoe that allows for a sock, but Connor insisted that the flip-flops worked just fine. We bought these flip-flops at Old Navy over a year ago, so I was surprised this morning when they still fit him.

"There are two clementines in your lunchbox, Connor," I say as he gets out of the car in front of Small Bunbin Academy.

"Thanks, Mom."

"You're welcome, sweetheart."

"Thank you for driving me to school."

"You're welcome, sweetheart."

"And thank you in advance for driving me tomorrow."

"Of course, sweetheart."

My husband, Haolio, is still cleaning the garage when I get home, so I park halfway up the driveway instead. With springtime in full bloom, he decided it was a good time for a deep-clean, and I agreed. The garage is the final part of the house in this endeavor, and is also the most cluttered. We rotate the clothes in our dressers and closets seasonally, to maximize drawer space and prevent overly-futuristic outlooks. Haolio found an extra bin of attire for warm weather that we missed when we did our quarterly closet rotation last month. Connor was overjoyed when his father carried the surprise bin into the living room, immediately searching for his 'lost' Superman flip-flops.

"Here they are, son," Haolio said, holding up the blue pair.

"Thanks, Dad. That is great." Connor took the flip-flops from his father, and slipped them right on.

I open my car door and step onto the pavement, waving to my husband, who has his hands filled with many forgotten lampshades. "Hi, dear!"

"Hello, Jeanine! I am sorry for the mess. Cleaning out the garage is turning out to be a much larger task than I imagined."

"Thank you for cleaning it, dear. Is there anything

I can do to help?"

"Actually, there is," Haolio says as he puts down the box of lampshades and walks towards me. "If you turn to your left, you'll see that I have placed a treadmill on our front lawn."

"Yes, I noticed when I pulled up to the house. Where did you find a treadmill and why did you decide to put it on our lawn, Haolio?"

"Well, Jeanine, if you look further towards the house, you will see that I attached a long wire to an even longer extension cord-"

"Where did you find an extension cord that long, Haolio?"

My husband comes to me and holds my hand, then says, "I don't want to alarm you."

"Even if you do alarm me, that is okay. We will work through it. I just want to know your reasoning behind the treadmill on the lawn."

Right as Haolio opens his mouth to speak, Connor comes flip-flopping down the sidewalk. "Hi Mom! Hi Dad!"

"Connor, sweetheart," I begin. "Why are you not at school?"

"I did not have proper footwear for gym class, so instead of running with my class, I ran home to you both."

Before Haolio can react to our son's self-proclaimed early dismissal, Connor slips off his Superman flip-flops and hops onto the treadmill.

"His little legs run so fast," Haolio says, still holding my hand.

Connor increases the treadmill's incline. Behind him, fairy lights hung haphazardly across the garage ceiling flicker on. A rainbow baby bonnet and a bouquet of forget-me-nots rest atop one of the many boxes.

# John Sheds

When Bob asked his wife, Martha, why she loved stormy weather, she told him that the rain felt nice on her face. Bob thought this was a funny answer, because when they had a leak above Martha's side of their bed, Martha complained. She assured her husband that his confusion was understandable, but he has confusing opinions too. "Popcorn and tortilla chips," Martha said. "They are both made from corn, Bob."

"That is a great comparison, Martha, since I enjoy popcorn, but am not a fan of tortilla chips."

"That's right, Bob. These are the quirky parts of us that make us who we are."

"I completely agree, Martha."

Bob and Martha bought their house on Faded Valley Road from Susan and Janice, who never noticed leaks. Susan and Janice explained to Bob and Martha about how they both have skin that is desensitized to moisture, due to their years living at the humid base of the El Yunque Rainforest. The first leak that Bob and Martha experienced took place in the shed that stored Bob's shovels and hoes.

Bob patched the small hole in the roof of his shed without any trouble. "What a relief, Martha," he said.

"I know, dear. We don't want any rust to form on your shovels and hoes."

Storms proved to be a prime example of how two truths can both exist and contradict. When it rained, Martha's smile grew brighter; she was cast as the understudy for the sun. Also when it rained, more leaks appeared in both Bob's shed and Bob and Martha's - previously Susan and Janice's - roof. Bob patched every leak as soon as he could, not wanting anything to turn storms into negative events for his wife.

During the first rainstorm after Martha's passing, Bob picked a handful of dandelions near the base of his shed. He felt raindrops on his neck as he laid the flowers against the steel. As he reached for his cane as he stood, Bob caught sight of a corn snake in the grass. Bob laughed, thinking about popcorn and tortilla chips, then rain and leaks. His favorite brand of pre-packaged popcorn was from a brand called *John's*

*Cob*. Because of this, Bob named the snake John. A few blades of grass over from John was his recently shed skin; he slithered centimeters away from a layer of himself. Bob often found himself jealous of snakes.

# Railroad Signs

Papa told Mama that he thinks it is time to move to a new house. I heard them talking the other night; I was in my bedroom upstairs, with the door cracked open, and they were downstairs in the living room with the local courthouse livestream playing at a low volume on the television. The doorknob on my bedroom door creaks when I turn it, so I leave my door ajar at night in case I need to open it further, so as to not wake my parents with the squeaky knob.

"Why, Joseph, would you like to move to a new house?" Mama replied.

"Because of the train, Patrice."

"I guess it *would* be convenient to live so close. Young Marcus could ride the train to school on days when driving him would be inconvenient."

"Young Marcus would gain a sense of independence

57

from that experience," Papa said. "I am glad we are on the same page, Patrice."

"Surely, Joseph. I am curious what Young Marcus will think of this idea."

I removed my earplugs and opened my already open door. "I am coming downstairs to discuss this plan further," I called.

"Why, Young Marcus," Mama said. "Papa hopes to move closer to the train. Do you like the sound of that? You could ride the train to school occasionally."

"Papa, what was the origin of this idea? What was the primary cause for you to want to live near the train so suddenly," I asked.

"That's a fantastic question, Young Marcus," Mama said.

"Well, Young Marcus, Patrice," Papa started. "I had a dream about railroad signs."

"Which ones in particular?" I asked.

"Last night, it was the mustard yellow, diamond shaped sign, with one solid black, vertical strip down the center, and a criss-crossed strip intersecting the solid black one diagonally."

"I know that railroad sign," Mama said.

"That is not the only railroad sign I have been dreaming about, Patrice," Papa continued.

"What other railroad signs have you been dreaming about?" I asked.

Papa inhaled slowly, his belly inflating like a balloon as he sat there, all air-filled and oxygenated. "Two weeks ago, I had a dream about the upside down T-shaped, black and white sign. The one alerting passersby of how many tracks there are. This one said '6 tracks.'"

"That is a lot of tracks, Joseph."

"Young Marcus, Patrice," Papa began. "Have either of you ever dreamt of railroad signs?"

Mama and I were silent for many hours, considering Papa's question until the sun began to rise. "I haven't," Mama said.

"Me neither," I said.

She poured me a glass of chocolate milk and handed me a bowl of banana oatmeal. Papa left his mug on the counter before racing to work before we had a chance to answer his question. Mama rinsed and dried the mug, placed it back in the cabinet. "I have never dreamt of railroad signs," she repeated.

"Me neither," I said again.

# Logging Out: Website Update

Enough people inquired about changing their settings to no longer 'accept all cookies' for it to pop up on the Frequently Asked Questions page. I was alerted to fraudulent activity on my credit card, immediately canceled the card, signed up for a new one, and logged on to replace my old credit card number. Changing my credit card information was relatively easy, though secure enough where I did not worry about this situation occurring again.

After clicking on 'payment details' in the little blue button's drop down menu, I had to type in my password for the website in order to see more than just the last four digits of the card number saved on file. The last four digits of my new credit card number reminded me of my old credit card number, the first and last of the four being the previous number plus two, and the middle numbers of the four last numbers being flipped. My heart dropped as I stared at the two different credit card numbers; I was not ready to say goodbye to the old one.

This sadness quickly turned to anger, then to longing, then a sort of grief. I did not like the 'tap' feature on this new card, as it added another decision to any in-person purchase: swipe, insert, or tap. Just that morning, I was at the grocery store and couldn't decide on the sweet Italian or spicy Italian for my chicken sausages. I shuffled through my mind's rolodex of sausage recipes, visualizing how the flavors would fit in with the other ingredients. After half an hour, I decided to scratch the decision all together and buy kielbasa. By the time I made it to register, my mind was still spinning from the spontaneity of my choice, so to then have the option to swipe, insert, or *tap* my new credit card sent me over the edge.

The kielbasa memory crashed over me as I my mouse hovered over the 'remove card' button. I reached in my desk drawer and pulled out my daughter's old flip-phone. The battery was long gone, but something about holding the scratched plastic with the numbers worn off the buttons - I could finally breathe again.

I went into the little blue button's drop down

menu and clicked on the FAQs page. I scrolled down the generous list of information, hoping to find an answer, and then noticed the search bar above all of the Frequently Asked Questions.

*Can I keep a canceled credit card on file?*

No answer came up, but a message did, matching the generosity of the long list of information and updated security regardless of payments.

*Don't see what you are looking for? Contact us here.*

I reached for a sticky note and wrote a reminder to myself to contact the website about my unanswered question, and that I don't need to worry about removing my old credit card until I have a definitive answer from them.

Appreciative yet again for their consideration, I scrolled through the FAQs one last time. That is when I noticed the newly frequent-enough question about changing the cookie policy. I returned my mouse to the little blue button's drop down menu, hovered over 'Log Out,' but could not get myself to leave yet.

Printed in the USA
CPSIA information can be obtained
at www.ICGtesting.com
CBHW031927090924
14062CB00001B/1

9 798218 459642